DR. TANJA P. HIGHTOWER

Destiny Grabbers

Copyright ©2018 by Dr. Tanja P. Hightower

All rights reserved. No part of this book may be reproduced, copied, stored or transmitted in any form or by any means – graphic, electronic, or mechanical, including photocopying, recording, or information storage and retrieval systems without the prior written permission of Tanja P. Hightower or HOV Publishing except where permitted by law.

All Scripture references are from the King James Version (KJV) Public Domain. All rights reserved.

HOV Publishing a division of HOV, LLC.
www.hovpub.com
hopeofvision@gmail.com

Cover Design: HOV Design Solutions
Editor: Dianna Knox-Cooper
Editor/Proofreader: Amy A. Owens

Visit the Author Dr. Tanja P. Hightower at:
www.tphightowerint.com
Info@tphightowerint.com

For more information about special discounts for bulk purchases, please visit www.hovpub.com

ISBN 978-1-942871-43-9
Library of Congress Control Number: 2018955124

10 9 8 7 6 5 4 3 2 1

Printed in the United States of America

DEDICATION

To Dr. Cindy Trimm and Lisa Nichols, for unloosing my mind and giving me the freedom to grasp my destiny and run with it. I thank you, Dr. Trimm for your teaching on the *8 Stages of Spiritual Maturation* that opened my eyes to maturity in all areas of my life. Thank you, Lisa for inspiring and transforming my thinking to grab hold of abundant living to speak with my authentic voice, and to write my story. You both have molded me into the person I am today. Thank you.

To my husband, Dave I appreciate the love and care you demonstrated in holding our family together while I pursued my destiny. To my children Daria and Dave Jr., you are my legacy and I pray that you fulfill your destiny with purpose and passion to be who you were created to be. Thank you all for giving me the space I needed to apprehend destiny. I love you!

ENDORSEMENTS

I am Charles Campbell, Rice University graduate, Husband, Father, licensed and ordained Minister, District Business Manager in Women's Health, Pfizer.

I have known Tanja for over 3 decades. As a devout Christian man, I have observed and admired the tenacity and dedication that Tanja has demonstrated for spiritual growth. She has put into action a commitment to getting to know God, His plan for her life, and his commission to share with others. Over the years I have witnessed her ongoing transformation from an aggressive worldly individual (as many of us were), to a Passionately God focused believer.
I expect big spiritual things out of Tanja through God! Writing this book is just the beginning!

Charles Campbell
District Business Manager
Pfizer

Dr. Hightower is a light that shines on dark and sunny days. I have reached out to her on a few occasions and have been embraced and humanized by her efforts in assisting others through leadership and mentoring. Dr. H and I worked together as regulatory investigators where she made my on-boarding worth its weight in gold. My experience was priceless working in conjunction with Dr. H for over a decade.

Dr. H and I later connected with Skillz Choice AAU basketball organization which was started and developed by me, but a key ingredient was missing until the leadership and the presence of Dr. H appeared. Dr. H brought a buffet of knowledge, compassion as well as mentoring as an assistant head coach for a boys only youth organization. She led our team and provided true grit when grit was needed, and passion came from the heart.

Dr. H is a diamond already buffed, shined and ready for display in the premium section no discount needed. Going forward any organization that Dr. H contributes to its foundation will certainly last a lifetime. I have always felt that Dr. H granted the community a gratuitous and enigmatic personality that never borders on selfishness.

Sincerely,

John Rutherford BS, RS, SHEP, CESCO
CEO/Owner
U-BETSafety since 2007

To my beloved sister in Christ, Reverend Dr. Tanja Hightower. Words cannot express how proud I am of you. From the first time I met you there was a zeal, humbleness, and a beautiful spirit in you that captured my attention. I saw you strive for perfection in the body in Christ. The race is not given to the swift but those who endure to the end. And it gives me great joy to call you my friend, my sister, my co-laborer in the gospel of Christ. I will forever cherish our friendship until the Lord calls us from labor unto reward. May God continue to bless you, your family and your ministry!

Reverend Ray A. Franklin
Liturgical Team
The Church Without Walls

A true leader has the confidence to stand alone, the courage to make tough decisions, and the compassion to listen -Douglas MacArthur

Dr. Hightower has been a steadfast leader when exercising and sharing her faith.

Dr. Deborah Stewart
Associate Superintendent
Fairbanks Independent School District

TABLE OF CONTENTS

INTRODUCTION 1
Created To Be

CHAPTER 1 3
Abandonment (Who's My Brother's Keeper)

CHAPTER 2 7
Child's Play (Helpless Without Fault)

CHAPTER 3 16
Young And Grown (Insecurities)

CHAPTER 4 25
Reaching But Not Enough (Rejection)

CHAPTER 5 40
Identity Crisis (Identity)

CHAPTER 6 54
Snatched Out Of Bondage (Destiny)

CHAPTER 7 65
Leading To Influence (Maturity)

CHAPTER 8 76
Imprint (Legacy)

CHAPTER 9 80
Empowering To Purpose (Inheritance)

CONCLUSION 89

DECLARATION & AFFIRMATIONS! .. 90

NOTES 92

ABOUT THE AUTHOR 94

Destiny GRABBERS

Introduction

Created To Be

At birth, we have no idea what our journey or destiny will be. When the earth was formed, there was the Creator of the universe. After the earth was formed, then the Creator made man in His image. Humanity was created with purpose. We were all created to be fruitful and multiply. *Fruitful* meaning production and *multiply* meaning increase and lacking nothing. If we were created to produce, then anything that is non-productive is in opposition to living a life of abundance. If *fruitful* means *producing* and *multiply* means *increasing,* we are always accelerating. We are all on a journey.

If we were created with purpose and created in the Divine's image, then the only One who can give us our identity is the One who created us. Moreover, the only One who knows our destiny is the Creator. If we want to know our purpose and destiny, then we must be connected to the source of creation, the One that can give us direction, instruction, and revelation of our destiny. John Ruskin stated, "Every person confronts three great questions. Where am I from? Whether am I going? And what must I do on the way?"

Having been created to produce and multiply indicates that we were created to have fellowship, family, and community. Our purpose is not for us alone. Purpose is always about someone else. In pursuing destiny, we must encounter pain that pushes us to a passion that leads to purpose and ends in destiny. As a result, we must be convicted enough to move past our hurt and grab hold of our destiny. Dr. Cindy Trimm states, "Your soul knows the terrain to your destiny".

In Proverbs 23:7 it says, "*As a man thinks in his heart so is he.*" Our intellect, our emotions, our beliefs, and our minds are the beacons to the directions we are traveling. What we know, how we react, and what we think can catapult us to the destination at which we will eventually arrive.

In being Destiny Grabbers, we must know the truth of our reality and be certain of what we believe. Find the truth, and we will find what we believe. Truth resides in the identity of who we are. If we don't know who we are, there is a possibility that we don't know the full truth of our purpose for living. The authenticity of who we are is who God, or our Divine, says we are. Find the truth of who we are, and we will find our purpose here on earth to reach our designed destiny.

CHAPTER 1

Abandonment
(Who's My Brother's Keeper)

From infancy to adolescence, I don't recall a close attachment to either of my parents. My mother became pregnant with me when she was a senior in high school. After she found out she was pregnant, she and my father got married. She was only 18 years old at the time. Shortly after she graduated, I was born. We lived in Houston, TX in Third Ward, which is called 'The Hood.' It was also the headquarters for the civil rights group called, *The Black Panthers*.

A year later, my mother gave birth to my brother. A year and a half after, my parents divorced. Shortly after my parents divorced, they each remarried someone else. My mother soon became pregnant with my youngest brother. She was married to my stepfather for 18 months and then divorced. Two years later, she remarried again and became pregnant with my baby sister. So, for the first six years of my life, my mother was married three times! Three years later, she divorced my sister's father.

My biological father was not involved in our lives very much after he remarried. In fact, it was about 4 years after he and my mother divorced before I saw him again. We

ABANDONMENT

soon found out that his wife did not like us. So, I believe, for my father to keep the peace in his home, he stayed away.

On occasion, while we were visiting our paternal grandmother (his mother), he would stop by to drop off the child support payments for my mother. He would visit with us for a few minutes, then he would leave. Although my brothers spent a few nights at his home, I never did.

After my mother's third divorce, we began to spend a lot more time at our grandmothers' houses. My mother would go out with her friends every weekend and because we were not old enough to stay at home by ourselves, she would leave us with one of our grandmothers. My siblings and I began to spend the weekends at either my maternal grandmother's house or my paternal grandmother's house.

One thing I want to say is that my mother raised us the best she knew how. I would later learn that she and her mother had some issues which, I believe, led to her behavior as an adult. My mother and grandmother did not have the typical mother-daughter relationship and the cycle continued between my mother and me and siblings. I would like to call the cycle, "emotional abandonment."

My mother and I never bonded. I don't recall any warmth from her that encouraged me to have self-acceptance, confidence, or assertiveness to be a woman of strength, power, and success. I can only remember having rules and confrontations when neither I, nor my siblings, followed the rules.

ABANDONMENT

As we grew, my mother was not around us all the time. However, when she was there, she had strict rules when it came to discipline in the home. I remember my youngest brother getting whipped with an extension cord or a plastic jump rope because he was always acting out and getting into trouble. Part of that discipline was instilled in her by my grandmother, who was practically raising us. Perhaps my mother and her mother didn't have a warm mother-daughter relationship because of their own pain.

"You know the definition of a dysfunctional family, don't you? It's any family with more than one member in it." **Sarah Pekkanen, <u>The Opposite of Me</u>.**

Although my maternal grandmother was not always a saint, she was the reason for the spiritual foundation in our lives. She took me and my siblings to church on a regular basis. We not only went to church on Sunday, but we went during the week as well. She had us in Sunday school, Baptist Young People's Training Union (BYPTU), choir rehearsal, and all scheduled usher board meetings.

I can truly say that if it were not for my grandmother, my siblings and I would not have grown into the disciplined, respectful, and successful adults that we are today.

Not having my mother and father to instill love, parental attachment, and connection in my life left me feeling emotionally abandoned. As children growing up, emotional abandonment can lead us to develop issues with low self-esteem. I later found out that it was the reason for

ABANDONMENT

some of my many failed relationships. Having had an issue with abandonment as an adult resulted in my being angry, having mood swings, and being involved in several unhealthy relationships. As a result, the Destiny Grabber of emotional abandonment caused a number of unhealthy and failed relationships.

In studying Counseling, John Bowbly's *Attachment Theory* is his belief that early relationships with the caregiver play a major role in child development and continues to influence social relationships throughout the child's life into adulthood. Bowbly's *Attachment Theory* suggests that children are born with a need to form an attachment.

CHAPTER 2

Child's Play
(Helpless Without Fault)

I can recall my first day of school in 1st grade. As soon as my mother dropped me off, I cried. I felt a sense of loneliness and abandonment from her again. "Why is she leaving me here?" "Why is she leaving me again? I thought to my 6-year old self. "Why can't I go with her?" My mother drove away, never looking back to see if I was okay. This was an extremely frightening experience for me. As I walked to my classroom, I continued to cry. My teacher noticed I was crying, walked over to where I was and began to console me. She hugged me and encouraged me by telling me that everything would be okay and to not be scared. This crying spell that I was having went on every day for the next few weeks. Eventually, I got used to it and didn't cry anymore.

In my 1st grade classroom, I sat at a two-seat wood desk table and a little boy sat next to me. Two little girls sat at the other two-seat desk table adjacent to us. It appeared that four children were sitting at one table. Under each desk, there were drawer compartments attached as well.

I don't remember much about the two little girls, but I have some memory of the little boy. Although I can't recall his name, I do remember him befriending me. He was the only child in my class who showed any interest in me. He was meeting an emotional need that I did not get from my mother or any of the other children in my class.

One day during class, he put his hand under my dress. He then put his fingers through the side of my panties and began to rub my vagina. He did this for just a minute or two, and then he stopped. I don't remember being mad, angry, or upset with him about it. Although he did not fondle or touch me every day, he touched me several times during the week.

I never told anyone about these 'touching/fondling incidents.' I honestly did not know if what he was doing was wrong or not. He was the only so-called "friend" I had at school. I do know that I enjoyed his attention.

During the summer, leading up to my second-grade year, we moved to another part of town. I eventually blocked the little boy and the 'touching/fondling incidents' out of my mind. In fact, the memories only resurfaced when I began to write this manuscript.

According to the DSM-V, Dissociative Amnesia consists of localized or selective amnesia for a specific event or events; or generalized amnesia for identity and life history. With selective amnesia, the individual can recall some, but not all, of the events during a circumscribed period of time (APS, 2013). Because of my selective memory, it was a possibility that I suffered from this disorder.

CHILD'S PLAY

We moved to the suburbs in a predominantly white neighborhood. My mother was still married to my baby sister's father at this time. There were just a few black families who lived in our neighborhood including some of my step-father's cousins. They lived about a mile away from us. My stepfather worked at night, so this gave my mother "free" time to go out partying with her friends. She would take us over to our older cousin's house about twice a month to spend time with them. My boy cousins were older than the girls, so they would be responsible for watching us.

One evening, while visiting with my cousins, all of us girls went into the bedroom to play. We all were lying in the bed with the covers over our heads. Suddenly, one of my younger girl cousins put her hands inside my panties and started fondling and penetrating my vagina with her little fingers. Here again, I was experiencing the exact same thing that I had experienced with the little boy at my former school. I was thinking this was a natural thing to do. The rest of my girl cousins were fondling each other's vaginas just as mine was being fondled. There was no violence or threat intended, or at least I did not sense it. We all were just playing under the covers. However, I never touched anyone of my cousins in that way. It was just done to me and I did not stop it, nor did I tell an adult about it. These fondling activities happened every time I visited with my cousins. Now as an adult, when I think about those incidents, I realize that my boundaries had been violated. I was introduced to this sexual act at a very early age.

CHILD'S PLAY

As I stated earlier, we lived in a predominantly white neighborhood. The elementary school that I was enrolled in was a predominantly white school as well. However, several months later, other black families slowly started moving into our neighborhood making it predominantly black.

Prior to the neighborhood becoming predominantly black, I distinctly remember a certain house on the corner a few houses from where we lived. A tall, older white boy lived there. Because our school was within walking distance from our neighborhood, my younger brother and I walked to school. Every day we had to pass the house on the corner where that white boy lived. I was in the second grade, and my little brother was in the first grade.

One day, as my brother and I were walking home from school, we passed by the house on the corner where the older white boy lived, and he began to bully us. Every day, he would threaten to beat us up, so consequently, we would run home from school daily to avoid him. It was–quite terrifying to walk home from school, knowing we had to pass the house on the corner and see the tall white boy who taunted us daily. Sometimes, instead of running, we would try to sneak by the house to get home.

Because there were only a few blacks living in the neighborhood, we had no one to help us and that made our plight more frightening. We never told our parents about the taunting and bullying that we encountered. However, one weekend when we visited our cousins, I told my older boy cousins about the tall white boy who was bullying me and my younger brother. They were in junior high school and I figured they could do something to stop the white boy from bullying us.

My cousins left school early one day and walked us home. That day was the best day of my life because our cousins confronted that older tall white boy. They grabbed him by the shirt and beat his ass. They also told him that if he ever threatened and bullied me and my brother anymore, they would beat his ass again. The white boy was so frightened that he never taunted or bullied us from that day forward.

The next year is when my mother and my step-father (my baby sister's father) divorced. My mother and her four children moved back to Third Ward "in the hood." While living in a single-parent home, my mother who had only a high school diploma, managed to get us on welfare. We were supplied with government cheese, green stamps, and food stamps. I was in the third grade, and I remember that my mother drove a white Plymouth. It had a hole in the floor on the passenger side. Those were hard times, but we made it.

We sometimes don't want to look at our past, but our past is the catapult to our future. We have to own our past to get to our future. We must search ourselves. The truth will set us free to fulfill our Creator's designed destiny for us. If we don't know our true identity, we will find ourselves on a different journey that is opposite of the created destiny that our Creator set before us, even while we were yet in our mother's womb.

CHILD'S PLAY

As children, we know only what we have been taught. We know only what we know and what we adapt to until someone says, "That is not right." So, as adults, what do we do when these hidden and suppressed emotions begin to resurface? What do we do when they suddenly overtake us and begin taking control of our lives?

I can recall now, that the little boy never told me not to tell anyone. This leads me to believe that in my subconscious mind, maybe I got pleasure when the incidents happened or maybe I thought what had taken place was normal. As an adult, I suffered from insecurities and experienced much rejection. I allowed others to control my life and almost steal my identity. Although I couldn't control what happened to me as a child, as an adult, I can control my today and tomorrow. That which we don't pay attention to today could be the result of our unfortunate yesterday. When we let others control our life due to insecurities and rejection, the result is Destiny Grabbers!

"Life can only be understood backwards; but it must be lived forward." Spoken by Soren Kierkegaard.

Christ died for my dysfunctional childhood. Isaiah 53:5 says, "...*take solace in the good news: He was wounded for my transgression, he was bruised for my iniquities.*" According to the Strong's Dictionary, '*transgression*' in the Hebrew language is 'pasha' which means guilt, punishment, or rebellion against godly living. Also, according to the Strong's Dictionary, the word 'iniquity' in Hebrew is 'avah,' which means to be twisted or perverted.

CHILD'S PLAY

As a second-grader, I didn't really know what godly living was. I also was not aware of what perversion was. Nevertheless, according to the Word of God, Christ took on my transgressions so that I could come to the knowledge of my wrong behaviors. He also did that, so I could turn from my troubled past and move toward my future in a positive way.

Ephesians 2:4-5 indicates *"Because of his great love for us, God, who is rich in mercy, made us alive with Christ even when we were dead in transgression it is by grace we are saved"* (NIV). My environment and actions of yesterday do not signify who I am today. Christ died that I may have life. Some things make us a product of our environment, but most of what we become stems from the choices we have made. I believe, that even as a child, I had a choice to tell somebody what that little boy or my cousins were doing. As I stated earlier, no one ever told me not to tell.

Choices determine courses. What happens on the course during the outcome of the excursion? The journey at times can be repulsed to the point of conceding promise. Difficult things can happen during the course of your journey that can hinder your path to your destiny. The race is not given to the swift but to those who endure. There must be a crushing of the oil to occupy promise. Jesus' agony for a moment caused him to think about refuting destiny, but He reverted to the promise at hand and succumbed His will to the Father's will according to Matthew 26:38-39.

CHILD'S PLAY

"But until a person can say deeply and honestly, 'I am what I am today because of the choices I made yesterday,' that person cannot say, 'I choose otherwise.'" Stephen R. Covey, **The 7 Habits of Highly Effective People: Powerful Lessons in Personal Change**.

We, as adults, can appear to be as exquisite as a teacup on the outside, but if the substance on the inside of the cup is tasteless, then the entirety of the cup loses its value. We must not allow our substance of untapped potential to cause our cup to not be put on the top shelf. We can't allow the substance of bitterness, insecurities, and unforgiveness to cause our cup to become flawed, damaged or lose its fervor.

Our substance must be that of purity, wholeness, and forgiveness. We are a top-line teacup that God made, and we have a purpose which will allow us to be positioned in royal places. We will not allow the attractiveness of the outside of our cup to override the value of what God wants to put inside His precious cup.

"REMEMBER YOUR GREATNESS."

Before you were born and were still too tiny
for the human eye to see,
You won the race for life from among
250 million competitors.
And Yet, how fast you have forgotten your strength,
when your very existence
is proof of your greatness. You were born a winner,

CHILD'S PLAY

a warrior, one who defied the odds
by surviving the most gruesome battle of them all.
And now that you are a giant, why do you even doubt
victory against smaller numbers,
And wider margins? The only walls that exist, are those
you have placed in your mind.
And whatever obstacles you conceive, exist only because
you have forgotten what you have
already achieved."

Suzy Kassem,
Rise Up and Salute the Sun:
The Writings of Suzy Kassem

CHAPTER 3

Young And Grown
(Insecurities)

In elementary school, I was attracted to boys, but they were never attracted to me, so I consumed myself in basketball and watching TV. I would see the other girls teasing and messing around with the boys. At that time, it was no big deal to me and I don't remember feeling bad about it.

While growing up, I was always bigger than the other children in elementary school because I liked to eat. I was tall and athletic which further explained my overeating. As I got older I, began to struggle with being overweight, which also caused me to have very low self-esteem.

I never had any close friends, however, on some occasions when I went to the park there was one other girl there. She and I would play basketball with the boys. Because I had no role model of how a little girl should have behaved, I adapted the role of a tomboy. I oftentimes played touch football with my little brother and his friends and believe it or not, I was the quarterback!

It was not until junior high that I fell under the social influence of wanting to date and having my first boyfriend.

YOUNG AND GROWN

Because of the lack of nurturing, abandonment, and alienation from my mother and father, one can assume that I was indeed emotionally abandoned. As I got older, my mother began to leave my siblings in my care and I shouldered the responsibility of being left alone with my siblings and running the household; I did not have a normal childhood.

When I entered junior high school, I focused my attention on achievement because I no longer had youth and immaturity to hide behind. If it were not for my playing sports, I would probably have been much bigger than I was because I was an "emotional eater." I loved cheeseburgers, and all chocolate, whether it was candy, chocolate milk, chocolate cake, or chocolate brownies. If I was not playing basketball, I was watching TV and drinking chocolate milk along with eating a cheeseburger.

Desperately wanting to be like the other girls, I tried out for the cheerleading. With my being overweight, you can imagine how that attempt turned out. I didn't make the cheerleading squad and I felt so embarrassed. I knew I didn't have a lot of rhythm back then, not to mention that I couldn't do all the flips and turns.

Eventually, I stopped focusing on being like the other girls and focused my attention more on my school work. While I was doing that, a tall, slim yellow-boned basketball player started flirting with me in my art class. He would make me laugh and always buy me things. We became girlfriend and boyfriend in the 7th grade. We were together every day during school and even ate our lunch together.

After a while of us dating, we began to skip school. He lived directly behind the school which made this extremely convenient for us. There was a fence separating his house from the school. We first started leaving school during our lunch break then, we started skipping the last period of the day, so we could be together at his house and have sex. I was 13- years old and he was 14.

On the days that he had basketball practice, he would usually come over to my house. I fell in love; mind you, I didn't really know what love was since I never had it. So, when that special someone showed love to me, I grabbed it. We were so in love that when my mother would go out, he would come over and we would top the evenings off having sex and more sex!

We would have sex in my mother's queen-sized bed. I chose her bedroom to have sex in because it was in the very front of the house and I could easily look out the window to see if anyone was coming into the house. One day while we were having sex I started to bleed, and the blood leaked onto my mother's sheets. At the time I didn't know why I was bleeding. I didn't know which made me more scared, the reason I was bleeding or that it had gotten on my mother's bed.

My boyfriend, being more experienced than me, told me that he had "busted my cherry." I later found out that my hymen had broken and that was what had caused me to bleed. The hymen is a thin piece of tissue that covers the opening of a female's vagina. Even after that frightening experience, every chance we had, we continued to have sex. We would even have it while we were sitting in the living room talking and my mother would be in her room!

I would wear some large culottes' that could be moved to the side, and I then sat on top of him while we had sex. I was not taking any birth control pills, and I was afraid to tell my mother that I was having sex. Remember, we were not that close. My boyfriend never wore a condom. So, when he was about to ejaculate, he would pull his penis out of me so that the semen would not shoot inside me. I always had a bath towel or a paper towel nearby for him to clean himself off after we were finished. I would go to the bathroom and wash myself off.

Because we were together so much I became jealous, and my insecurities got the best of me. I was so insecure that I became possessive and began to go through mood swings because I had a fear of losing him to the other girls.

I had no doubt that his love was the same as mine because he had some dysfunction in his family as well. His mother had passed away when he was a little boy and his father was an alcoholic. As a result, he was raised by an uncle and an aunt who loved him dearly. However, they really didn't care much for me.

YOUNG AND GROWN

In the two-story house where he lived, he had very little supervision. He lived on the second floor in a 'mini' apartment that was equipped with a small living room, a bathroom, a kitchen, and a bedroom. His uncle and aunt hardly ever checked on him, which was another reason we were able to freely have sex at his home as well.

We were loving each other out of abandonment; each of us was yearning to be loved and consequently, we acted out sexually. We had sex every chance we could. Eventually, these sexual episodes led to my getting pregnant at age fifteen; my boyfriend was sixteen.

At this time, my academics were exceptional, and I was on the Honor Roll. We both spoke to our families about my pregnancy. My mother and my grandmothers agreed that I had too much potential to have it be ruined by motherhood and they unanimously decided that I would have an abortion. However, my boyfriend and his aunt and uncle wanted me to keep the baby. I eventually decided that my education was more valuable than me becoming a teenage mother and my mother scheduled an abortion.

Even if I had wanted to keep the baby, I didn't feel as though I had a 'true' say-so in the matter. I knew that my mother would not help me take care of my baby because she wasn't really taking care of me or my siblings in a nurturing way. I also knew that I wanted to go to college and that me possibly becoming a mother would stop my chances altogether. My father never knew about the abortion.

"Since the earliest period of our life was preverbal, everything depended on emotional interaction. Without someone to reflect our emotions, we had no way of knowing who we were." John Bradshaw, **Healing the Shame that Binds You**

At the time we decided on the abortion, I didn't realize that having an abortion would leave me with the *spirit of abortion.* It seemed that everything I tried to start and finish, I aborted. It was as if I never could bring things to completion. My ministry, my dreams, my vision, my business investments, and my relationships were all aborted. I eventually almost aborted my destiny by using drugs and drinking alcohol.

The spirit of abortion was just another tactic that the enemy was trying to use to destroy my destiny and keep me from knowing my purpose. Ephesians 6:12 states, *"For our struggle is not against flesh and blood, but against the rulers, against the authorities, against the powers of the dark world and against the spiritual forces of evil in the heavenly realms."* Because we are spirit beings, demon powers are always going to try to stop us from fulfilling purpose through distractions and loss of focus. Demons do not have authority. Christ won the war as he hung on the cross and thereby took all authority. Matthew 28:18 states, *"All authority has been given to me in heaven and earth."* The only way demons can get authority is if we let them in by leaving portals open. I opened my own personal portal by having an abortion. In one of the Ten Commandments, God clearly states, "Thou shall not kill."

YOUNG AND GROWN

Being raised in the church, at age 15, I didn't think of the many ramifications stemming from killing my baby. All I could see was that I was an Honor Roll student and my education would be over if I chose to not have an abortion. That spirit of abortion also gives us that feeling of not wanting to deal with your problems; instead, we just ignore the problem, but it never goes away.

"Abortion of potentials is a massacre of purpose. You don't get the fruit because you killed the seeds!" Israelmore Ayivor, **Leaders' Watchwords**

After 30 years of wrestling with the guilt which mercilessly clung to me for having had an abortion instead of the baby, I could finally believe that the gift of the Holy Spirit did, indeed, abide in my life. However, this belief came gradually and sometimes agonizingly. I had to first receive God's forgiveness; then His healing power came, which enabled me to rebuke and to command the spirit of condemnation to leave and never return.

In a case such as mine, the first step in dismissing the spirit of abortion was to admit that I had aborted that which neither I nor anyone else had the right to abort. Next, I had to admit that only God, and He alone, could provide the healing needed to remove the lingering pain and heal the aching wound. After this step was taken, I asked God for the ability to forgive myself and then to seal this self-forgiveness with His peace. Finally, finding myself emboldened by God's overwhelming love, I commanded the hold of the spirit of abortion to be broken through my progeny. I commanded it to lose the hold it thought it might still claim on my body and to never return!

After the abortion, my boyfriend and I went to separate high schools giving me the opportunity to talk to other guys at my school. I ended up sleeping with one of the football players while I was still dating my boyfriend. This indicated that I still had that emotional tie to abandonment; I was still searching for love in the wrong place and in the wrong way. I believe that the permissive acts were the result of the rejection and abandonment I experienced during my childhood.

The good news is that I kept my grades up and I was able to participate in volleyball and basketball. I continued to be permissive with the football player while staying focused on the plan my mother and grandmothers wanted – getting enrolled in a college. I was later inducted into *Who's Who Among American High School Students*, The Health Club, and The National Honor Society. I graduated from high school with a grade point average of 3.8 and was ninth in my class.

Just as we sometimes search for love in all the wrong places, we may also run here and there in search of the wrong endeavors. We run like a swift she-camel in search for success without Divine Guidance. God owns the cattle on a thousand hills. He can give us the desires of our heart according to His will for our life. He wants to plant us in vineyards that we have not sown. He wants to plant us in fertile ground that we have not tilled. He wants to plant us in choice cuts, but we cannot be the one to lead. He says, "Follow me," and He will satisfy our souls and bring us into success and companionship.

"People think a soul mate is your perfect fit, and that's what everyone wants. But a true soul mate is a mirror, the person who shows you everything that is holding you back, the person who brings you to your own attention, so you can change your life.

A true soul mate is probably the most important person you'll ever meet because they tear down your walls and smack you awake. But to live with a soul mate forever? Nah. Too painful. Soul mates, they come into your life just to reveal another layer of yourself to you and then leave.

A soul mates' purpose is to shake you up, tear apart your ego a little bit, show you your obstacles and addictions, break your heart open so new light can get in, make you so desperate and out of control that you have to transform your life, then introduce you to your spiritual master..."
— Elizabeth Gilbert, **Eat, Pray, Love**

CHAPTER 4

Reaching But Not Enough
(Rejection)

My grandmother attended Prairie View A&M University, a historically black university located in Prairie View, TX, in the 1930s; she encouraged me to apply there. I applied and was accepted into the Mechanical Engineering Degree Program.

Coincidently, several of my high school classmates were also accepted at Prairie View A&M University. Me and two of my classmates, who both ranked higher than me in our graduating class, decided that we would be roommates.

When we moved on campus, unbeknownst to me, my two roommates had made the choice that we would be suitemates with two more girls from another high school. The four of them already had a very close relationship and shortly after we moved in together, they began hanging out together without including me. Because I felt left out, I decided to move into another dorm room with other former high school classmates.

Although my new roommates were not as high-ranking in high school as the first two, they were at least cooler and inclusive of me. These new roommates allowed me to "let my hair down" and be myself. We attended parties on Thursday nights and on the weekends if we didn't go home to visit. I stopped going to church and became socially expansive with my friends. I began drinking alcohol daily, smoking marijuana, and having casual sexual relationships with guys. Consequently, my grades began to slip. Nevertheless, I continued with this undisciplined behavior.

My first roommates not including me in their "hanging out" activities took me to my past and brought back the emotions linked to my abandonment. At that time, I was still not aware that I was suffering from rejection and insecurity issues. These issues continued to follow and affect me throughout my college years and into my adulthood.

"Over the years, I have come to realize that the greatest trap in our life is not success, popularity, or power, but self-rejection. Success, popularity, and power can indeed present a great temptation, but their seductive quality often comes from the way they are part of the much larger temptation to self-rejection. When we have come to believe in the voices that call us worthless and unlovable, then success, popularity, and power are easily perceived as attractive solutions. The real trap, however, is self-rejection. As soon as someone accuses me or criticizes me, as soon as I am rejected, left alone, or abandoned, I find myself thinking, Well, that proves once again that I am a nobody.... [My dark side says,] I am no good... I deserve to be pushed aside, forgotten, rejected, and abandoned. Self-rejection is the greatest enemy of the spiritual life because it contradicts the sacred voice that calls us the Beloved. Being the Beloved

REACHING BUT NOT ENOUGH

constitutes the core truth of our existence." Henri J.M. Nouwen

A time comes when we will have to confront all our old belief systems, persuasions, deliberations, decisions, choices, behaviors, methods, associations, assimilation, and conglomerates. We cannot intertwine the old with new ideologies, prospective, dispositions, persuasions, adjudication, determinations, convictions, confidence, attitudes, and new productivity if we want to be successful. Is there something new that is pressing on your heart, but it appears that you can't move forward? Then, consider that there may be some old habits, behaviors, or ideologies that are suppressing your progress. What is your Destiny Grabber?

I didn't seek professional counseling until later when other symptoms occurred such as mild depression and a mixed disturbance of emotions. These feelings and thoughts were very real in my life but as a child, I didn't know that these emotions were buried inside of me and needed to be rooted up. I didn't know that this incident was a problem in my life and was pushed deep inside of me, causing my real authenticity to be camouflaged.

I immersed myself in the Word of God and the fellowship of other believers to gain strength and power to overcome these habits daily. I am not saying this method is for everyone, but this change is what saved me from self-destruction. I thank God that he delivered me from drugs and alcohol. I overcame the negative components of Destiny

REACHING BUT NOT ENOUGH

Grabbers and accepted the positive components of Grabbing Destiny.

While pursuing my second Master's degree at Lamar University in Beaumont, TX, I studied Clinical Mental Health Counseling. Some of the symptoms of this disorder are substance-related disorders that include alcohol or other substances. For me to be delivered from drugs and alcohol, I had to detach myself from that environment and get around positive people.

During the summer before my senior year, instead of securing an engineering internship like my other classmates, I chose to go home to work at a pizza place. While working there, I met a guy who became my regular sex partner. And that is just what it was…. SEX! I was not ready to commit to a relationship and neither was he. He shared an apartment with two roommates; one was male, the other was female. Sometimes I would go out clubbing on the weekends with his female roommate. I would go back to their apartment drunk, have sex with my 'sex partner,' spend the night with him, and then get up and go to work the next day.

When summer was over, I went back to college but instead of living on campus I shared an apartment with a roommate. I completed college and earned a degree in Mechanical Engineering. I was so proud of my accomplishment and although I graduated with a 2.7 GPA, that did not matter to me! What mattered was that I'd finished college!

REACHING BUT NOT ENOUGH

After graduation I was back home living with my mom, we still did not have the mother-daughter relationship that I longed for. We did not get along well at all. Although she was telling me what to do and what not to do, I felt that I was grown and did not have to listen to her. This did not help our relationship at all. It made things tense between the two of us.

Shortly after my graduation, I was granted an interview in Bethesda, Maryland at a naval base. The naval base sent me a round-trip plane ticket, paid for my hotel, and provided the proper amenities during my stay. My interview went very well, and they requested a copy of my official college transcript.

After they received my transcript, I received a letter informing me that they had chosen another candidate to fill the position. I never found out the "real" reason since they don't usually disclose that information, but I knew in my heart that the job had been offered to be someone who had a higher-grade point average than I did. I just knew that they didn't want to take a chance with an employee who had a "C" grade point average.

My classmates who had decided to do engineering internships the prior summer, were all granted jobs after college. Their employment made me feel worthless and like a failure. I had made an unwise choice to return home the summer before and now it was coming back to haunt me. I also credit my not getting the engineering job to my wanting to fit in therefore hanging around the wrong people.

REACHING BUT NOT ENOUGH

Unlike my peers, I never landed an engineering job. I ultimately went back home to live with my former 'sex partner' who later became my boyfriend. The lease with his other roommates had ended, so he had moved into his own apartment. I could not afford my own apartment at that time. I started back working at the pizza place and I also started selling vacuum cleaners part-time. About a year later, I was hired by Harris County in the Mosquito Control Department where I served 11 years. I later transferred to the Health Department where I worked for an additional 7 years as a Health Inspector. Although it was not an engineering job, it paid more money than I had ever made and provided excellent benefits.

I made enough money to finally move out and live on my own. I also purchased a brand-new car. These changes gave me a chance to live what I thought was the best life. I was living on my own and could do what I wanted to do, go where I wanted to go, and come home when I was ready. I went clubbing every night with two of my former college classmates and I was still able to get up and go to work the next day. I was "being me" but did not really know who I was.

Two years later, still being the *Boss Lady* of my own life, I got pregnant by my boyfriend. Our relationship was not stable at all. We would break up and get back together and the cycle continued repeatedly. You would think that pregnancy would stop me from going to the club, but it didn't. I had an emotional need to be with my friends and although I lived alone, I did not like being alone. I had

REACHING BUT NOT ENOUGH

formed an attachment to my friends and when we were together, I always had fun. My boyfriend and I were not that close, and I believed that it may have stemmed from my issues with abandonment.

"Children who feel unloved and unprotected are like a half-filled cup. They become incapable of 'filling up' because they have come to believe they are unworthy of love. They try to please others, give to others, and care for others in a desperate hope that they may make themselves worthy." Beverly Engel.

During my pregnancy, my maternal grandmother, the one who practically raised me and my siblings and me when our mother would go out, was diagnosed with terminal lung cancer. She was the one who instilled Christ in me and laid the spiritual foundation in my life. She was the one who took us to church practically every day. She was one of the main people who not only told me she loved me, but also showed me true love.

When my grandmother was soon transferred from the hospital to hospice, I visited her daily until my seventh month of pregnancy. The doctors notified my family that she was quickly declining and would be given morphine continually to keep her as comfortable as possible.

Seeing my grandmother at the end stages of life was too devastating to me. My family decided that because of my pregnancy, I should not visit anymore. A few days later, one of my relatives called my job to tell my supervisor that my

REACHING BUT NOT ENOUGH

grandmother had died, and they were coming to pick me up. I felt a loss when my grandmother died; it was as though a piece of my heart had been torn away.

Inevitably, storms will come in our lives. I recall while living in Houston in 2017, Hurricane Harvey really created a disruption in our lives. It took 2 1/2 hours to get to work and 3 hours to get back home, a great change from a normal day which would normally take 30 minutes.

As I sat bumper-to-bumper, I heard the Lord say to me, "Persevere." He said, "Will you withstand the results of the storm. The storm has passed but not without leaving vast interruption, disturbance, or disorder to your life. Can you tolerate the agitation until the end? Can you allow me to rebuild, revamp, recondition, and refurbish your life so that I can use you for my Glory and catapult you into a promise?" We must learn to withstand the storms of life and allow God or our Divine Source to restart the process of pushing us into our destiny.

"We live in a world that is beyond our control, and life is in a constant flux of change. So, we have a decision to make: keep trying to control a storm that is not going to go away or start learning how to live within the rain." Glenn Pemberton, Hurting with God.

Three months after the passing of my grandmother, I gave birth to my daughter. But her birth didn't leave me in a great state of mind. Although her father and I co-parented, we lived separately as he stayed in his apartment and I stayed in mine.

Missing my grandmother and grieving her death, I returned to drinking alcohol and smoking marijuana. Eventually, the marijuana and alcohol were not enough to suppress the emotions of grief I was going through. I started mixing crack with my marijuana, creating a mixture that is called "primo."

I had chosen to not enroll my daughter in daycare and I took her to her father's house or my other grandmother's house every chance I got. By this time, my father had come back into my life, and he started watching my daughter at least twice a week. At that time, I didn't realize that I was following a pattern similar to the one that my mother had started with her children. I was going out and never spending time with my daughter.

I even remember one time when my daughter was about a year old and I couldn't find a babysitter. Some of my friends came over and we were smoking primo while my daughter was in her baby swing. I remember each time the swing stopped, I would wind it repeatedly, never picking her up. I later asked myself, "Am I my mother's daughter? Am I abandoning my daughter as I was abandoned?"

During that time, I didn't know, and to be honest, I didn't care. You know only what you know. My daughter's father saw that I was always on the go and he became extremely concerned about our daughter. He finally suggested that we live together again. He wanted to be able to keep a constant eye on our daughter and me. He also said that it would be a way he could keep me home and know where I was. He would allow me to smoke primo in the bedroom while he and our daughter stayed in the front room.

I had visited my paternal grandmother's church one or two times after my daughter's birth. One night I was in the bedroom getting high in the dark and I saw a vision of my deceased grandmother. She came to me and said, "I love you Tanja. You need to go back to church." When my grandmother spoke to me in that vision, it immediately blew my high. I began to cry and call out to God. I told God that if my cousin, who was a minister, preached on the following Sunday I would join the church and come back to Him. Even in my stupidity, I was bargaining with God. My belief was that if God was real, then He had to prove it to me by allowing my cousin to preach. If that happened, then I had no choice except to believe that he was calling me back home.

That Sunday at church, when it came time for the sermon to be preached, my cousin stood up to bring the Word. I sat there looking astounded because God had done His part! Now, it was time for me to do my part. When the announcement came that the "doors of the church" were open, it was as if I was pushed out of my seat. I ran to the front of the church and I rededicated my life to the Lord. I had initially gotten saved when I was 10-years old.

REACHING BUT NOT ENOUGH

My returning to church didn't stop me from smoking primo and drinking alcohol. There is an understanding of spirituality and accepting Christ in your life. When a person accepts Christ into his or her life, there is a renewal of his or her spirit only at the confession. Although I had accepted Christ at age 10, my body and mind had not changed. Only my spirit changed. Remember that we are created in the image of God, and He is a spirit.

I continued smoking primo and drinking alcohol. One day, I was at my girlfriend's house, and she was getting ready so that we could go to the club. It was raining, thundering, and lightning. I was in the living room rolling a primo when a loud, enormous thunder sounded, and a long streak of lightning hit while her patio door curtain was open. I was able to see God do His work.

When that lightning struck, and that large thunder rolled, it frightened me so badly that I thought it was God trying to tell me something. Something inside told me to tell my girlfriend that I had rededicated my life to the church and there was going to be a time when I was not going to be able to smoke, drink alcohol, or go clubbing anymore.

I eventually stopped going out and smoking primo and continued to go to church. I was serious this time. I told my baby's father that I could not live in sin anymore. He was not ready to get married so he moved out. He was able to get an apartment in the same complex that I stayed in and that made it easier for us to begin co-parenting again.

REACHING BUT NOT ENOUGH

In the process of living in my own apartment, going to church, and raising my daughter, I met this younger guy who had a daughter the same age as mine. This situation gave my daughter and me the opportunity to go to events with him and his daughter. One day, my daughter told her daddy that she had gone to the carnival with mommy's friend and his daughter. So, my baby's dad asked me who my friend was and why I had our daughter hanging out with him and his daughter. I told him that the guy was a friend of mine who had a daughter the same age of our daughter. My baby's daddy didn't like that answer and made up his mind that no other man was going to raise his daughter. Mind you, he had told me that he would never marry, so I made up in my mind that I was never going to marry him.

On, November 22, 1990, we spent Thanksgiving Day at my paternal grandmother's home. My baby's daddy told the family that he was going to marry me! I was in another room at the time he made the announcement. When I came back into the room where everyone was, they told me that my boyfriend was going to marry me. In disbelief, I asked him if what they were saying was true. He confirmed that we were indeed getting married.

I never got the traditional proposal that I had always wanted and maybe I should have asked my boyfriend for it. I see now that I set the standard for our marriage because I didn't demand the respect of him asking me the traditional way a proposal should have been made. I believe now that by accepting a lower standard of a marriage proposal, I

REACHING BUT NOT ENOUGH

accepted what was given to me because I was so happy that he was going to marry me. I accepted his "proposal."

I wanted so badly to get married and have someone change the way that I had allowed myself to be treated. We married on March 29, 1991 and although everything went well for us the first couple of years, I was not happy. My husband stopped 'dating' me. He stopped taking me out to dinner and he became a 'homebody.' I, however, still had "the run" in me. I started going out with my friends again. I ended up having an affair because I was not getting the attention that I wanted or needed. I was still trying to fulfill the emptiness of love and abandonment and My affair lasted a year without my husband ever finding out about it. Later that year, after ending the affair, I was received a job promotion and a raise. This allowed my husband and I to purchase a house in the suburbs and when we moved, I decided that I was going to do better and focus on my spirituality. As soon as I made up my mind that I was going to focus on family and my spirituality, I became pregnant with my son in 1994.

We must understand that people will treat us the way we allow them to treat us. We also have to remember that out of fear, we will allow certain circumstances or events into our lives. When we fear, we allow the fear to feed information into our belief system or our minds. Fear can put us into action, or it can slow us down. Destiny Grabber! I allowed fear to control my actions and accept the way my present husband said he was going to marry me instead of suggesting to him to ask me the traditional way. I allowed my insecurities and fear of abandonment to push me into getting married on someone else's term rather than on my term. Fear may be caused by several things such as insecurities, a lack of control, revenge, or even greed. When decisions are made from fear, a person misses the logic of the situation, and he or she does not base the decisions he or she makes on facts.

"Women's Empowerment Reminder of the Day: Always respect yourself as a woman. You attract what you are, so be very mindful of how you're representing yourself. If you want respect, you must first learn how to respect yourself first. Attracting negative attention is never a good thing. Be a woman of substance! Be a woman that both women and men respect, admire, and look up to. Don't disrespect yourself by lowering your standards and accepting just anything that comes your way. It's okay to be single! If you want a relationship of substance, you can't keep entertaining people and things that mean you no good. Think about it! It's all up to you." --- Stephanie Lahart.

I watched a television series called "The Underground." One character I thought was interesting was a house slave named "Caido." Caido, at one point, was the top house slave. Years later he became one of the area's wealthiest free slaves. I said "free" slave; however, as a slave, he really was not free. He took many trips to Paris, and there is where he met his wife.

He returned to America with his wife and a bounty slave catcher wanted to reverse Caido's status. The bounty slave catcher threatened to kill Caido's wife if he didn't give him information on the Underground Railroad or help catch Rosalie. She was a woman who assisted Harriet Tubman with the Underground Railroad.

Caido manipulated his circumstances to work in his favor in the house where they kept the slaves; he learned all the hidden tunnels. He intentionally hurt himself so that John Brown's wife could help him recover and find out information. John Brown was a white lawyer who also helped slaves escape. When his own people found out what he was doing, they shot him on the courthouse steps.

When John Brown's wife found out who killed her husband, she was both angry and hurt. Caido took advantage of her feelings and told her she had two choices; to deal with "Fear" and to keep it in or to let it out. His philosophy was to let it out by taking control and taking revenge. Caido was so fearful that later he turned on his own kind to have control.

In 1996, I moved my membership to a church that was pushing me to grow, and in 1998, God called me into the ministry. I was involved in various church ministries and bible study classes. In 1999, I enrolled in seminary, and in 2000, I went to serve and start a church plant.

CHAPTER 5

*Identity Crisis
(Identity)*

For years I walked around lost and not knowing my purpose. I knew what I was called to do, but I didn't know why I was put on this earth. When we don't know our purpose, we tend to serve someone else's purpose. Have you ever helped someone fulfill their vision day after day, year after year, and suddenly one day you realize you have a vision of your own?

My service in the ministry started out great. I was attending seminary and began to learn in depth more of what the scriptures meant. I began to understand and fulfill the call on my life as I became an associate pastor in 2000. I was given the title Evangelism Minister. I was excited to be able to serve and have a title. I served in this role for about a year, and then became a part-time staff person as the Mission Pastor in 2001.

While serving as the Mission Pastor, I had the opportunity to really utilize my gifts of witnessing, teaching, and preaching. I oversaw the Evangelism Ministry, the Nursing Home Ministry, the Bereavement Ministry, the Kerygma Ministry, and the Outreach Ministry. I implemented outreach initiatives, structured ministry

IDENTITY CRISIS

guidelines and procedures, and conducted training and development of leaders, staff, and preachers.

Although I was called into the ministry in 1998, I wasn't licensed until 2002. In 2003, I lost my job with the county which opened up the opportunity for me to become a full-time staff person as the Mission Pastor. Once I became a full-time staff person at the church, I began to be emotionally and verbally abused by my leader. Because I had lost my job and was working in the ministry full-time, I felt like I had no other place to go; I stayed despite the abuse I was receiving. Let me just say that I believe nothing happens by coincidence.

I continued to serve just as I had always done from the beginning. I continued to teach discipleship classes. One thing that gave me great joy was seeing my pupils grow into the persons they were created to be. Seeing their lives change became my passion, as was making disciples of my pupils. I desired for them to recognize the true identity of who they really were and find out for what they were created because by doing that, they would have to intimately know The Creator. I would ask them what their passion was and what gave them joy without them even trying to do it.

When I taught my discipleship class, it was to cause transformation. I didn't just teach my class to be informative. I taught my class as a facilitator with interactive participation. I believe when everyone in the class is interactive, it gives room for conviction and inner healing. That, in turn, is what leads to transformation. I was teaching

IDENTITY CRISIS

my class from the book titled *Breaking Free*, authored by Beth Moore.

It seemed as if everyone really enjoyed my teaching style and my class became very popular in the ministry. I would ask my pupils to reflect on what was being taught and what they got out of it. Sometimes, by asking them to do that, they would receive a personal conviction. My pupils were between 30- and 50-years old.

My employer, who was also my leader, was teaching another class at the same time my class was being taught. His pupils were younger than mine and he was teaching on a totally different subject than I was. He and I had two very different personalities and teaching styles. My pupils never had to worry about their issues or concerns being discussed outside of the classroom and certainly not in an upcoming sermon!

When students left my class, they were extremely excited, and they continuously talked about how effective the class was. Well, word got back to my employer and he became jealous. He started using his authority and power to make me look bad. He began to belittle and ostracize me, and other people stopped speaking and talking to me because of him. After all the sessions for my class ended, I was not allowed to teach that or no other class again.

I still continued to serve. Even though I was working in a full-time capacity as the Mission Pastor, my assigned duties became sweeping and mopping the floors, vacuuming

IDENTITY CRISIS

the carpet, and cleaning the toilets. I was not even allowed to preach on Sunday mornings. Instead, I was assigned to preach only during Wednesday Night Bible Study. Even when my leader would travel out of town, a guest preacher would be brought in for Sunday morning services instead of me being allowed to preach. Yet, I also performed all of the other duties required to keep the ministry going. I felt that if I was not good enough to preach on a Sunday morning, why was I good enough to preach on some Wednesday nights?

My sister and brother-in-law had joined the ministry a few years after I did. Although my brother-in-law was a licensed minister, at that time he had not yet been ordained as a pastor by my leader. However, my leader did allow him to preach on Sunday mornings.

The fear of rejection is proximal to abandonment. The primary reason for fear of rejection can come from low self-esteem and this fear is often demonstrated when we look to others to make us feel better or when we constantly seek approval from others. We must remember that suffering rejection oftentimes leave us open to the possibility of something more demanding, such as manipulation.

The manipulation started and the divisiveness of turning other ministers against me mounted. The looking behind my back became second nature. I had to be careful of what I said to others in the ministry because the snitches would go back and tell him everything I said. This became the norm instead of the unusual. It became so stressful that it began to affect my health.

IDENTITY CRISIS

During a health fair that I was hosting on behalf of the ministry, I decided to have my blood pressure checked by a nurse who was serving there. My pressure read 160/140 and the nurse told me that I needed to make an appointment with a doctor right away. Although I was working full-time in the ministry, I did not have insurance and that just made me even more stressed. The nurse told me that she knew a doctor who would see me at a discounted rate and when I eventually went to see the doctor I was given a prescription for blood pressure medication.

I remained in the ministry at the church for as long as I could. I dealt with the manipulation, intimidation, and the emotional turmoil daily. I continued to keep my mouth closed and watched every little thing I said in the meantime. Looking behind my back to see who was watching me was pure hell in the church house. I did not have any friends and it seemed that all the members were loyal to our leader. My own sister turned her back on me. She never came to my rescue or took up for me during the entire ordeal and it left me hurt and heartbroken.

I made up my mind to look for outside employment. After filling out several applications, I was finally called for an interview with the State of Texas Department of Corrections for the position of Parole Officer. The interview went well, and I eagerly expected a call back from my interviewer to offer me the position.

One Sunday morning in March 2005 while at church, I was called by the head deacon into the room where the

IDENTITY CRISIS

deacons and preachers met prior to service. He informed me that the leader was sitting me down from leadership because I was not emotionally able to lead. In that moment, I heard God clearly say to me, "It is time for you to leave. There is nothing left for you at this church." However, I still couldn't believe that after five years of serving this establishment by giving my time, talent, and treasures, I was being treated as an outsider.

In serving someone else's vision for all those years, I got lost in the person's vision and lost myself. I allowed myself to be controlled, manipulated, intimidated, and abused emotionally and verbally. I allowed myself to become weary, angry, frustrated, and emotionally uptight because I was taught to serve other people's visions first. How then, could my vision ever come to fruition?

When we are unclear about our purpose we will allow ourselves to labor in another man's field too long. After a while, we will become frustrated to the point that our mind becomes confused and our mind becomes cloudy. Sometimes we have this battle going on which asks, "Should I leave, or should I stay?"

Have you ever been in a place too long? If so, chances are that you became agitated because you knew that you were worth more. It is like you knew that there was more inside of you and that you have your own vision but, you were afraid to move, fearing what others would say. Then you realized, "Something has got to give!" Don't let Destiny Grabbers of Fear reign in your life.

IDENTITY CRISIS

"Never forget what you are, for surely the world will not. Make it your strength. Then it can never be your weakness. Armor yourself in it, and it will never be used to hurt you." George R.R. Martin, **Game of Thrones**.

I did receive the call from Texas Department of Corrections Parole Division to start work at the academy on April 5, 2005. A week before it was time for me to report to the Parole Officer's Academy to train for the job, I called the leader to set up a meeting. I was going to hand in my letter of resignation from the church. I was led to turn in my letter of resignation because I was not going to allow my insecurities, abandonment, diminishment of character, demeanor, hurt, heartbreak, or betrayal stop me from fulfilling my purpose.

My desire to serve faithfully was taken advantage of by my own doing. I could blame others, but ultimately, I am responsible for my own actions. We have a tendency to devalue ourselves, and when we devalue ourselves, others tend to devalue us as well. We get only what we give. This was the choice I made.

Have you noticed that if you don't play life, life will play you? Are you willing to let life play you by helping someone who does not value you? Are you willing to continue to work for someone else when you know there is greatness inside of you and when your purpose is calling you?

IDENTITY CRISIS

When I arrived at the church for the meeting, my heart was pounding, and my hands were sweating. I didn't know what was going to transpire. My leader didn't know what was going to happen either because he had one of his bodyguards meet me and stand by the door while we had our conversation. After turning in my resignation, I was told by my former leader that I would never work full-time in ministry again.

These words were daggers in my back. I never thought I would receive this type of treatment when I was called by God to the ministry. All I wanted to do was serve God, give my all to help others, and to fully know the God I serve. Nothing more, nothing less.

When we hear negative feedback from someone we love, look up to, and give our time, treasures, and talents to, we may feel weak, unworthy, and hurt to the core. Especially while facing the consequences of neglecting family, marriage, children, and self-care.

Have you ever had someone tell you that you would never be able to build your business, be successful, live in the house you want, drive the car you want, speak before thousands telling your story?

I left that meeting feeling dead inside. I was literally thinking I would never work full-time in ministry, be successful, or fulfill my purpose and I cried all the way home. I figured the best part of what had happened to me was that man didn't put purpose in me. Man didn't call me,

IDENTITY CRISIS

and man didn't create who I am and who I will become. I knew there was something greater for me to do.

We are not a result of peoples' opinion of who we are. We were created for purpose. We were created and uniquely made to do something extraordinary and designed specifically for ourselves. How many of us have a dream or vision and have allowed insecurities, fear, and failure stop us from moving forward?

I had lost the awareness to be who I was created to be. I knew such treatment was not what was purposed for my life. In serving someone else and wrapping my full self into their vision, I should not have never been treated with such disrespect and betrayal, nor suffered from high blood pressure. I truly thought I was doing right by serving someone else.

My insecurities wore me down and allowed me to be manipulated. My abandonment from childhood allowed me to latch on to someone who used me only to get what he wanted. When we don't know who we are, and we are detached from a parent at childhood or abandoned in a relationship, we tend to bolt ourselves to anyone who demonstrates a need for us.

Have you noticed that after you have given your all, (met quotas, made budget, cleaned the home, gotten the children to practice, stayed late, allowed your marriage to go on the rocks because of a job, children's grades failing, etc.) that your unappreciative employer, your faithless

IDENTITY CRISIS

companion, and your children are more concerned with these things getting done rather than considering what you want? Have you ever been betrayed by someone who was more concerned with their own agenda than how you felt?

I was so hurt and heartbroken because my leader turned my sister—my own flesh and blood—against me. My sister was more loyal to him than she was to me. This put a figurative nail in my coffin because I would have never thought my sister would betray me as well. This blow hurt me deeply. I later found out after I left, my former leader ordained my brother-in-law as a pastor.

Going through betrayal is a low blow, especially when we have put our confidence in certain individuals. We put people in positions in which they were never meant to be in our lives. We should never let a person have that much control over our lives. However, when we don't know who we are, we will accept anything.

Are you willing to take control of your own life? Are you willing to let go of other peoples' opinions of your life? Are you willing to love you for you? Are you willing to take your life back and walk in your own purpose?

I had been ostracized by my peers. I had been persecuted and accused of not being a team player. My good name had been slandered. When we try to fulfill the call on our lives, attempt to fulfill our purpose, or try to remain humble and respectful, we are often labeled as "rebellious," "insubordinate," and "misfits" in the ministry's

IDENTITY CRISIS

advancement, the company's growth, or to the relationship's development.

I left the ministry began my "fresh start" with new feelings of being alone, hurt, used, and taken advantage of. For the next seven weeks, I had to attend the Parole Officer Training at a prison under the State of Texas Parole. I had the opportunity to be with a lot of people who were 10 to 15 years younger than me; they were youngsters. After class, the youngsters would go to the local bar for happy hour. I didn't mention earlier that prior to my call into ministry, I used to drink alcohol to the point that it erupted into anger.

I started going to happy hour with the youngsters and returned to drinking to cover the hurt and the pain I was still feeling. I used the drinking to fill the void of rejection and brokenness. Sometimes, we tend to cover up the ripped heart and mask the shame of who we are, and who we have not yet become. We pretend that all is well. I covered up my low self-worth with self-pity with drinking.

We use the drug or addiction of our choice, whether it be alcohol, prescription drugs, street drugs, abusive relationships, insecurities, low self-esteem, anorexia, or overeating, to hide our true self. Have you ever been in a crowd and still felt alone? Raise your hand and know that you are not alone.

I hid the painful emotions to feel better about myself. When we are hurting, all we want to do is hide our feelings. We want to put up a façade or pretend we "got it all

IDENTITY CRISIS

together." We justify the hurt with substance whether it's with words or appearance. Are you willing to go through life miserable and alone? There is a difference between *alone* and *lonely*. *Lonely* is unattached or abandoned and *alone* is separated or lack of companionship.

I was lonely because I had been abandoned, rejected, not only by the person who employed me, but also by my flesh and blood sister. She was supposed to stand by me at all costs. I explained earlier how I was emotionally abandoned by my mother and father. We can sit amid a crowd and still be lonely. We can live in the home with family and still be detached emotionally. Are you amongst the crowd, yet lonely? Even during your loneliness purpose calls.

Purpose was calling me. I had the opportunity to encourage and empower the youngsters while we were together. This was also a part of my purpose. In the midst of my heartache, I was able to speak life, truth, honesty, purpose, and worth to them and help them find out who they were created to be.

When we have purpose, a calling, and destiny within reach, the Creator will not allow us to wallow in our mess, pity, or shame. He will create situations where our purpose will be used to help someone else and for us to grow into who He has purposed us to be. Have you ever noticed that you can have a problem but someone else comes with a bigger problem and you realize your problem doesn't look so bad? How many of us are willing to come out of self-pity

IDENTITY CRISIS

or the mundane to have a meeting with your destiny and make an appointment with your purpose? This is the denouncement of negative Destiny Grabbers and retaining the positive Destiny Grabbers of purpose.

After I graduated from the academy, all my pain and hurt, along with my emotional rollercoaster was turning into hope. We may fall, but we get back up. We may even fail, but our future comes out of failure. Will you turn your pain into gain or your insecurities into courage? If you are ready to start this journey and grab hold of destiny tell your neighbor, "The old house is vacant! I'm in my new house! Hello neighbor!"

At my graduation, as I walked across the stage, my peers applauded loudly and clapped enthusiastically when I received my Parole badge. I felt proud, blessed, and grateful. At my lowest, I was given the opportunity to speak life and strength and draw a map of purpose for my peers who appreciated me.

We never know when the opportunity will come to give back or impact someone else. We need to know that all things work together for the good. We need to know that if we stay the course, make the right decisions, fulfill our purpose, use our uniqueness to reach those goals designed for our service, and equip ourselves for the journey set before us, the race won't be as challenging. We must remember that life is a marathon and not a sprint.

IDENTITY CRISIS

Are you willing to be pushed into purpose? Have you reached your full potential? Has anyone helped you expand your capacity to be successful and gain the wealth you deserve? I am looking for individuals who are open-minded to creative thinking and ready to grab hold of their ordained destiny and "impossible" dreams. Are you ready for greatness?

CHAPTER 6

Snatched Out Of Bondage
(Destiny)

In October 2006, I made a lateral transfer from Texas Department of Corrections to Texas Department of Family and Protective Services, also known as DFPS. This job was far more satisfying because my services in the church were limited, and I believed God had placed me at DFPS because of the kind of people I would encounter daily.

Don't get me wrong. I loved working with parolees and assisting them with their transition back into society. However, my position at the Texas Department of Corrections didn't pay me enough financially. The job at DFPS gave me the opportunity to minister to a broader range of people, such as the elderly, the disabled, and the mentally ill.

I believed for a long time that, when the opportunity presented itself, God would use me in an unorthodox way to minister and help change these people's lives. Although it was a state job, whenever I felt the need, I yielded to the Holy Spirit and allowed my voice to be used to speak profound words of truth.

SNATCHED OUT OF BONDAGE

I eventually went back to seminary in 2007 and I was allowed to use the credits from my Master of Theology degree toward my Master of Divinity degree.

During all of this I began to realize that I was still bound by "religion" and old belief systems. However, in 2010, I traveled to the Caribbean Island of Barbados where I met Dr. Cindy Trimm, my mentor. I attended her Kingdom School of Ministry that led to my deliverance as I sat under her teaching. A semester's-worth of classes were truncated into a one-week course.

Dr. Trimm truly spoke life into my spirit during that week in Barbados. The revelation from the teaching helped me to understand that God had created family before the church ever started. The revelation I received also taught me to never neglect myself, my family, or my spouse because of the church. We are to serve God and not allow man to become our idol. I began to hear the voice of God clearly say to me that I was serving man and not Him. That entire week I cried, my nose dripped, the tears were so salty. I was becoming free! Free from "religion."

Dr. Trimm helped me to see that in order for me to change my way of thinking, I needed to "think big." Dr. Trimm stated that I was one decision away from my dream. She also stated that my feet could not go where my mind had never been. Dr. Trimm showed me the difference between the church and the Kingdom of God. I mean she really broke down the meaning of the scriptures straight from the Bible!

SNATCHED OUT OF BONDAGE

I visited several churches between 2010 and 2014. I was searching for the Kingdom of God in the church. One of the churches I attended was an Apostolic church which was a church that flowed in the supernatural through signs and wonders. I developed a deeper relationship with God; which led me into the prophetic.

In 2014, a friend of mine invited me to a women's conference that was being held at the church where I had been emotionally drained. However, I had been set free and healed from the leader of the church. In fact, I had seen him a couple of times at other functions due to us worshipping in the same arena. We were able to be cordial to each other. I had moved on and forgiven him and my sister. I knew that I could not succeed or walk in my destiny while holding onto unforgiveness.

I attended the church conference and my former leader acknowledged me from the pulpit! I was pleasantly surprised. I went to see him after the service was over. He hugged me and invited me back to the ministry. I told him that I needed to talk to my husband and to pray about it. Even though my former leader may not have known it, I knew I was not the same person I was when I left his ministry 10 years ago. My sister and brother-in-law were no longer members of the ministry. They left a few years after I did.

I made the leader aware that I was coming back. I explained to him that God had showed me that what I had learned and been through would help the church move to the next level. I rejoined the church after meeting with the leader and asking him what he expected of me and telling him what I expected from this ministry.

We agreed that I was not the same and he indicated that he was not the same either. He assured me that he was open to what God wanted to do through me to assist in the ministry. Although I was not put over a specific ministry within the church, things went well during the first and second years. It was not until 2016 that things began to change, and his actions reverted to those that caused me to leave his ministry years before.

When you have been through dysfunction, you don't forget what it looks like. During one particular Sunday morning, the spirit was so high, and people were being delivered. As the Holy Spirit was moving amongst the people, I went over to my leader and his wife and told him that this move of the spirit was the reason God had led me back to his ministry. It was my assignment after teaching a class and expressing the move of the Holy Spirit to bring on deliverance.

I sensed that the people had been hungry for Spirit of God to move. But my leader was so controlling that the members were scared and intimidated by him. Nevertheless, I followed what God told me to do. I was not afraid of him. I fear God more than I fear man.

I was not going to fall back into being manipulated, intimidated, or stressed out. I recognized the signs and decided that I was not going to put up with this type of behavior in my life again. I began to step back and just remain a leader because of my ministerial status.

When his fellow "conspirators" (the elders and the leaders board) saw that I was not going to fall back into that trap again, they decided to watch me again. They were also my leader's biggest supporters financially. So, when they started acting differently it was as if he was caught in between hearing and obeying God or listening to his leaders.

Remember, when I first arrived, I was on an assignment to help move the church to the next level. That elevation did occur to a point as long as the leader was cooperating with God's movement and not following his own agenda. Many signs showed me that my assignment was over and that I had done what God wanted me to do. Yet again, I stayed out of fear of not having anywhere to go.

Unfortunately, there are times when the assignment is over, we continue to remain because we believe we don't have anywhere else to go. I had forgotten that assignments are not forever, and I knew when I arrived, it was temporary.

"Never be afraid to trust an unknown future to a known God." Corrie ten Boom.

In the midst of fulfilling our purpose or on the road to reaching our destiny, there will always be distractions and detours that could lead to perilous situations or circumstances such as the loss of a loved one, the death of a marriage, the loss of job, the lack of finances, broken relationships, betrayal, hurt, and pain.

SNATCHED OUT OF BONDAGE

At just the right time, however, a miracle, a reconstruction, a rearrangement, a repositioning, or a renewal manifests, and God alleviates all the chaos. He rejoins that broken relationship, emancipates that lack of confidence, and gives restored birth to your vision. God restores your finances, restores your relationships, renews the gift of creativity, and gives you new innovative ideas.

My brother passed away on Sunday, January 1, 2017. That was the day that I experienced spiritual shipwreck. What a way to start the New Year! His funeral was held on Saturday, January 14, 2017 and some leaders came to the funeral out of respect for my ministerial position at my church.

After the funeral, when getting into the funeral car to go to the cemetery, I saw my leader walking up. I immediately got out of the car to meet him, but to my surprise, he walked straight to the car that my sister was in. She was not a member of his church anymore, yet instead of coming to give condolences to me, a member who was serving at his church, he chose to console a former member. I was very aware that my insecurities tried to flare up again, but that is a prime example of what he would do to make me feel unappreciated.

The next day, which was Sunday, my sister informed me that she and my brother-in-law were coming to my church service. I was later told by one of the other ministers that the pastor didn't want her, the minister, to sit by me. I would usually sit on the front row with the her and the other ministers, but because of the information I was given, I decided to sit on the second row.

A week prior to this, another incident had happened with the pastor involving another friend of mine. She abruptly left the church. Because she and I were friends, he thought I had something to do with her leaving.

While I was sitting in service, my sister and brother-in-law came and sat on the second row next to me. My emotions were high due the fact that I had just buried my little brother and to add to the hurt I was already experiencing, my leader started saying condescending things from the pulpit and it was just unbearable at that moment. He truly thought I had something to do with my friend leaving the church.

When he started saying catty things from the pulpit, it wouldn't take a rocket scientist to know he was throwing stones. My sister later told me that she knew what he was doing. The hateful words being flung from the pulpit made me even more aware that again my assignment was over at his ministry. I made up my mind to leave this ministry for good.

In February 2017, I went to Arkansas to hear Dr. Trimm speak. When I had attended her empowerment summit in December 2016, I learned that she had a program in which she would cover a person in ministry and I decided to ask her if she would cover me. After she was done speaking, she began signing books and when it was my turn for her to sign my book, I asked her if she would be my covering; she agreed.

Upon arriving back home, I received an email from my leader requesting a meeting with him, one of the elders, and the leader of the ministerial staff. The meeting was planned for February 12, 2017. However, on the prior Sunday, February 5th, after the first service had ended, one of the pastor's armor bearers told me that the pastor wanted to meet with me. My original thought was, *this is not the planned meeting day*. I was caught totally off guard and I was not prepared. I would normally pray before having a meeting with him, but this time I did not.

When I entered the meeting, there was my leader, his elder, the leader of the ministerial staff, and his head armor bearer. I sat down among them at the roundtable. I must be honest and say that I had my defenses up. In the email my leader had stated that only two other people were going to be at the meeting. However, his head armor bearer, who is also on his board, was in the meeting.

I felt overruled in anything I was going to say because it has four against one and I was extremely uncomfortable. When my leader questioned my intentions in ministry matters, I got off track and informed him that I was resigning from leadership. My leader became defensive and began to verbally abuse and insult me again.

He told me that I can't dress and that I had *just* started to dress and to "look like a preacher." He accepted my

SNATCHED OUT OF BONDAGE

resignation and the elder then stated that I am a person who does not listen. I tried to ask him a question and he quickly became defensive.

I went on to tell my leader that lately, when I entered the doors of the ministry, I felt as though I was dying because he was not able to give me what I needed to grow spiritually. The leader of the ministerial staff just sat quietly and listened to everything being said. I asked her directly if she understood what I was saying. She responded only by telling me that the meeting was not supposed to go as it did. She also stated that if I would have just listened, the meeting would have gone a different way.

I take full responsibility for not listening. But to be called into a meeting that was scheduled to be held a week later and get ganged up on by more people than originally scheduled, was a shock for me. My insecurities kicked in when the leader said that I didn't "look like a preacher." To me, a person with insecurities, that statement was an insult. It also implied that something was wrong with my appearance—my looks, and my weight. It provoked questions like, "Am I cute enough?" "Am I slim enough?" "What does a preacher look like?" To me, "not dressing the way the leader wanted me to dress," were harsh words to my ears. In essence, I heard him saying that I am worthless.

Although I was not prepared for the meeting, I do believe that everything happens for a reason. When I left the meeting, I was so hurt by all that he said that I sat in the sanctuary through the end of the second service, and then immediately left. I never returned.

I sent Dr. Trimm a notice to inform her of what had transpired and informed her that I was not going back and. She was scheduled to preach at my former leader's church on February 24, 2017, however, I knew that the dysfunction remained there, and I refused to subject myself to anymore torture. I closed that chapter of my life.

A choice made on appearance is not always where the blessings come. It is the anointing and power of God in your life that determines whatever choice, decision, or direction you should go. God will allow His blessings to progress or outpour if you have been seeking Him. "Seek ye first the Kingdom of God and all these things will be added."

Abram and Lot had to separate. Abram was at crossroad where he had to make a choice. However, he allowed Lot to make the choice for him giving him first priority on the land and he would take the land that Lot didn't want. Lot selected the choice land that appeared to promise prosperity, abundance, and plenty. Abram took what was left. Afterwards, God told Abram to look to the north, south, east, and west and that all the land he saw was his and his offspring's.

My point is that no matter what choice or decision we make, when we have the blessing, favor, and the anointing of God on your life, success, prosperity, abundance, and wealth is already afforded to us if we seek Him first.

CHAPTER 7

Leading To Influence
(Maturity)

"Your beliefs become your thoughts, your thoughts become your words, your words become your actions, your actions become your habits, your habits become your values, your values become your destiny." Mahatma Gandhi.

In March 2017, Dr. Trimm started teaching The 8 Stages of Spiritual Maturation. This course was designed to elevate the capacity to receive what God has for the individual who diligently serves Him. Another vital part of this process was learning how to access and develop key components of one's life.

The study of maturation stages has taught me that I can be 100% in my spirituality while still lacking in my family life, marriage, relationships, or finances. The 8-Stages of Spiritual Maturation teaching, along with Lisa Nichols' book, *Abundance Now* and her course, *Speak and Write to Impact*, has caused my life to take a 180-degree turn. Ms. Nichols describes the four types of speaking, which are Informational, Motivational, Spiritual, and Transformational. I have identified that I am a Spiritual and Transformational speaker; those qualities compliment my leadership.

LEADING TO INFLUENCE

I can grab destiny now because I truly know my purpose. I am on the road to success and abundance. I am grabbing destiny and not letting insecurities, abandonment, or rejection highjack my destiny. I am my own rescue. I am in control of my life and I can no longer blame anyone for the mistakes I have made or for my lack of accomplishing success. I was created to subdue, rule, and take authority over everything in my life.

Where you are planted and to whom you are connected have a massive impact on your advancement, enlargement, and improvement. When a tree is planted beside a stream, its roots will stretch to receive water and sustain its life. If we are *not* planted where living water is flowing, chances are that drought has struck the land. Some of us, surprisingly, may be planted near the stream and still suffer a drought. The Good News is that because of our physical closeness to the stream, even in our exhaustion from the heat and our scorching from the sun, we are still producing fruit. Remember that we are planted by the stream and thereby connected to the life-giving source of nourishment. This nourishment is the Word of God and the Holy Ghost.

Capturing the proper perspective of life can be complicated when we are not connected to the source. The force is the fire that keeps us going, the creator of our being, the soul snatcher from the demonic, and the giver of life. If we are on a path not compatible with the original plan for our life, then we are spinning our wheels and traveling a route that will delay promise.

LEADING TO INFLUENCE

When we don't know our identity, we tend to receive every voice, every idea, or thought that is placed in front of us and we may think it's from God. In reality, however, it may be a distraction. Try the Spirit *by* the Spirit to make sure you are on the course you should be on. You must not be unsettled in your mind. Our minds can become so cloudy and disengaged from the original plan that we may believe the 'wrong thing' is what we are called to do. The enemy can have you believing the wrong plan for your life. If you want to know the original plan God has for you, go back to your first love—Christ.

Think it not strange that the sinful nature will do what it is designed to do and what it wants to do. But as believers, we may someday be asked by God, "What did you do with the gifts I gave you?" "When I was hungry did you feed me?" "When I was thirsty, did you give me something to drink?" "When I needed clothes, did you clothe me?" "When I was sick, did you look after me?" "When I was in prison, did you visit me?"

God is the creator of all. In Acts chapter 10, while Peter was praying God was revealing to Peter that He does not show favoritism. We can get so caught up in positions, power, and authority that we may miss or deny the revelation that we were created in His image and that we are His workmanship. We are all included in God's plan to be some type of leader, even if it's leading our own lives. He has no respect of person.

LEADING TO INFLUENCE

A leader is required to pass certain requirements such as maturity, the development of character, integrity, and commitment. Leadership is being able to motivate or influence individuals toward an action in achieving a common goal. John Maxwell states that leadership is an influence. Leaders are also visionaries who see the future for their organization. Leaders inspire people into action and spend most of their time communicating and clarifying vision to their followers.

Because I was the oldest of my siblings, I have always been a leader. Even among small groups, I never shied away from sharing my opinions. I was the one who wanted to take charge, however, I was not always so confident. When I hit a low, my insecurities would not allow me to step up. I would hide in the background and would lead only if I was asked to do so. As aspiring leaders, before we can lead effectively, we must face our own demons. Once when we have gone through the process of maturation, we can lead others. My desire is to empower individuals to become leaders in their industries around the world.

"Don't follow the crowd, let the crowd follow you." Margaret Thatcher.

While sitting in a discipleship class, before being called into the ministry, I was the one that who was always inquisitive and asked questions. I loved to talk about things that I was passionate about. I always loved to talk about the Word of God and His people.

LEADING TO INFLUENCE

I remember teaching my first Sunday school class and giving leadership. The more I taught, the more I loved leading God's people into the truth and self-worth of who He said they were. I also gave leadership in teaching small group discipleship classes and vacation bible school. As you can see, my passion lies in teaching, giving and demonstrating leadership by empowering, encouraging, and enlightening others to fulfill their purpose and be who they were created to be.

My biggest joy came from two students, in one of my small-group classes, who were struggling in certain areas of their lives. They would come week after week and talk about their issues and how their strongholds had them bound. One of the students would come crying about her romantic relationship and how that she was being treated like dirt. She was so in love.

The other student was upset with having to always bail her children out of trouble. It was wearing her down. I empowered them with the Word of God. I told them both that they were victorious and strong. I spoke life to their situations and lifted them up with affirmations. I gave them a shoulder to lean on until they were able to stand on their own and take control of their situations. They knew that they had the power to change things and that they didn't have to let anything disrupt their environment. I was very proud of these young women, and it gave me joy to know that God used me to help them become powerful in who He created them to be.

LEADING TO INFLUENCE

My next leadership role occurred when I was able to assist in planting a church. This was a huge leap from teaching and discipleship in the classroom setting. This role began with me being appointed as evangelism minister who oversaw the Evangelism/Outreach Ministry that I referenced previously. I took on this role because the church was just starting, and someone had to take it. As a leader, I did what I could to serve. Although, I knew I was out of place, I realized that sometimes leaders are called to serve wherever they are needed.

As the years went by, I became frustrated because I knew this was not my passion; I only served because I am a servant leader. When you are not in purpose, there will be an uneasiness inside. Leaders are taught to persevere, remain humble, and give servant leadership even when we are in a role for which we are unqualified or feel uncomfortable. You must sometimes put your purpose on hold for the sake of the team. A leader always puts the team first. I continued to lead while frustrated, torn, and uneasy on the inside. However, I served with a smile on the outside

"As a leader and having to influence the people who you are leading, you must remember that they are looking to you to guide and lead them to new levels, a new start, or a new phase in life." (Maxwell, 1997)

The illumination shining on our faithfulness will prove our trust in a thing, person, or God. In the Hebrew, the word 'trust' means, "to be patient, assured, or confident." In our journey, a level of trust about what we see as our promise or whatever we are attempting to accomplish must arrive for us. Our confidence cannot waiver if we trust the finished product or harvest. Our faithfulness is our process of deliverance. Our trust is our assurance and confidence of the result. While being a leader, we must do what we can to gain the trust of our followers. And likewise, the followers must also gain the trust of their leader.

As a mission pastor, mentoring leaders allowed me to assist them in setting goals for their ministry, seeing what their needs were during the process, and also what lay ahead to grow the ministry.

A leader always demonstrates and communicates the vision of the more senior leader, manager, or the overall organization. My job was to help the ministry leaders incorporate their vision into the main vision of the organization, thereby, creating team responsibility to accomplish the common goal of the organization. A leader should also communicate what each individual leader needs to know to accomplish that vision. A leader needs to communicate the blind spots and point out what is working and what is not working, what is in line with the vision, and what is not in line with the vision. Lastly, a leader needs to know how to grow the organization.

Since growth is a process, everyone will not be at the same level. Some individuals need more development. Although the ministry has a long-term goal, the leader should identify short-term goals or attainable goals for the group. If the group is able to reach short-term attainable goals, it is more likely to have the ability to progress to the long-term goals.

As the years went by, my personal experience of leadership was not always glamorous. As I mentioned, it led to me suffering through jealousy, emotional stress, verbal abuse, and depression, and while there are some very good leaders out there, there are also some who are insecure and lack social skills. These shortcomings do not allow them to channel their emotions except with the people they are leading. It is often said that, *hurting people hurt people.* There are some leaders who allow their insecurities to get the best of them and cause division in the team. Some leaders do not know how to handle it when someone on the team has a different, and perhaps more powerful gift than they have. I was always taught that on a team everyone does not have the same gift; that is what makes a team effective. All are using their gifts for the common goal winning. Unfortunately, insecurities will drive one to abuse his or her authority because of fear.

Abusive or jealous leaders are fearful that the individual whose gift is more powerful than theirs will somehow cause them to lose control over the people they lead. They abuse their authority to let the other leader know that they are still the *head honcho.* This type of leadership is shown in I Samuel, Chapter 18 with David and Saul. "Whatever Saul sent him to do, David did it so successfully that Saul gave him a high rank in the army. This pleased all the people and Saul's officers as well. When the men were returning home after David had killed the Philistines, the women came out from all the towns of Israel to meet King Saul with singing and dancing, with joyful songs, and with

LEADING TO INFLUENCE

tambourines and lutes. As they danced, they sang: "Saul has slain his thousands and David his tens of thousands". And from that time on Saul kept a jealous eye on David."

"We should never pretend to know what we don't know, we should not feel ashamed to ask and learn from people below, and we should listen carefully to the views of the cadres at the lowest levels. Be a pupil before you become a teacher; learn from the cadres at the lower levels before you issue orders." Mao Tse-tung.

Most leaders who are insecure are controlling and are unable to lead effectively. The problem with having a leader with insecurities and controlling tendencies is the likelihood of attendant behaviors, stress, and depression on the victim person they are leading. As I stated in previous chapters, I suffered from this type of leader. At times, I didn't know if I was coming or going. Every time I came into the presence of this leader I felt as though I had to guard my heart and mind. I prayed to God to cover me. I believed that the depression overwhelmed me because I was torn inside. Nevertheless, everything I did for the organization I did it with a servant's heart and from a fervent desire to please God.

I thought I was doing what I was supposed to do in fulfilling the call of God on my life. God finally showed me that I was not really serving Him, I was serving man. And not only was I serving man, I was serving a man with insecurities. I was serving a man who took advantage of his authority and stated that I was in rebellion if I didn't do what the power structure wanted me to do.

LEADING TO INFLUENCE

I strongly believe that when I was accused of being 'rebellious', that brought on the stress, depression, high blood pressure, and the tormenting of my soul. Also, it was stated that I was "going against the ministry." That accusation tore my soul apart because I had given "my all" to the ministry.

As a leader, when you are told that you are "going against the ministry," it is a lonely feeling. Leadership can be lonely. I hear Jesus saying, *"If anyone comes to me and does not hate his father and mother, his wife and children, his brother and sisters, and yes, even his own life, he cannot be my disciple. And anyone who does not carry his cross and follow me cannot be my disciple."* (Luke 14:26-27)

When you love God, you do all you can for the ministry, but is it really for "the ministry," or is it "for man?" This applies to a secular organization as well. Our first obligation is to serve the common goal and to help others. But when we focus on pleasing one individual and that individual disappoints us, we will be hurt. A true leader is always leading for the common good of the organization. But most of all, he or she is obligated to lead with integrity and character. A leader who lacks integrity or character loses his or her influence.

God knows our heart. Our heart is connected to our mind. If the mind has not been renewed, then deception can invade the ear gate and affect the heart. Our heart must be searched daily. Out of the heart, the mouth speaks. Our heart will portray our character. Therefore, be diligent in keeping your heart pure and clean. David made the appeal in one of his Psalms, "Create in me a clean heart and renew a right spirit in me." I decree a pure heart.

"Integrity is within. Integrity is not "circumstances" but the choices we make that reveal character and good ethics. Our circumstances are responsible for our character. As a mirror is to our physical appearance, what we see in the spiritual mirror reflects who we are." (Maxwell, 1997).

Even in the situation with my leader, I had to search myself to find out what the Creator wanted me to work on. I can only speak for myself and assert that much as of the opposition I endured came because God wanted to develop my character. Even in serving, there were a sense of not belonging, abandonment, and insecurities. In spite of obtaining all the degrees I received, it only indicated that my credentials did not exhibit integrity. Credentials do not reveal who I am; only my character can do that.

John Maxwell stated, "Many succeed momentarily by what they know; some succeed temporarily by what they do, but few succeed permanently by what they are."

Chapter 8

*Imprint
(Legacy)*

"The things you do for yourself are gone when you are gone, but the things you do for others remain as your legacy." Kalu Ndukwe Kalu

When we are pursuing purpose, it should always be about leaving an imprint on society. To leave an imprint on society is to serve humanity. Serving humanity requires going beyond the norm and sometimes being the first to go against the popular. We must ask ourselves, "What am I doing to create change in the world? What am I doing as a game changer? What am I leaving for the next generation?" Our beliefs, values, and thoughts are what transcend to the next generation.

As I pursue destiny and walk in purpose, my desire is to serve others. Serving others is to reach inside their pain and disrupt their old habits, beliefs, and values to catapult them into purpose. My passion is to empower, encourage, and enlighten their spirits to journey toward destiny and touch the world. It is my desire to shake the memory and highlight others' dreams and visions to leave a legacy. Leaving a legacy or impression upon the world requires dedication and heart. Legacy will sometimes bring about

IMPRINT

scars, scars from leaving the past behind, scars of being rejected, persevering, and being alone.

"Dreams do come true, if only we wish hard enough. You can have anything in life if you will sacrifice everything else for it." J.M. Barrie, Peter Pane

There were days of loneliness and my not understanding what God was telling me. Everyone thought I was losing my mind and some people told me that I was emotional and needed help. It reached the point where I isolated myself a lot because I was afraid people would distract me from my assignment. In spite of their doubt, I never made a move on my dreams and visions. I never forgot them.

Once I started believing in myself and not caring what others thought, I began to pursue the dream that God gave me. He gave me a clear mind to break away from insecurities and rejection. My dream has always been to leave a legacy for my family and to empower others to be who they were created to be. I embraced the Destiny Grabbers of encouragement, empowerment, and enlightenment that catapulted me into purpose.

In completing this book, I am in the midst of answering the call on my life. I know that I am a communicator, whether from the pulpit, through one-on-one conversations with clients at my current job, or whether it be at a speaking event attended by thousands. Leading others to their purpose and pushing their potential to full realization

IMPRINT

of who they were created to be, is my passion. It is a passion which enables me to help others touch the world.

When we have purpose, an assignment, or call to greatness, God will place us in unfamiliar places so that our voice will cry out and authenticate the One Who called us. Our voice must be, and will be, heard by those who have an ear to hear what The Spirit is saying. It is amazing how God knows who needs to hear our voice. As a result, He will send the right people whose ears are the receivers of our voice. Think it not peculiar when strangers are placed in our path. It is because God has perfectly orchestrated destiny.

When the assignment comes, it means we must be ready to capture new territory. However, we first have to be directed by God. Next, we must realize that the new territory is a place of the unfamiliar; there will be obstacles, distractions, and delusions. But to advance, we have to be bold, courageous, and at peace that God is with us. Persistence leads to provision. Provision leads to peace, and peace leads to prosperity.

For some, assignments lead to the local church, community, city, or state according to the assignees' measure. Whatever the assignment, call, vision, or dream, the "called" must be obedient to it. As a game changer, history makers, and global leaders, assignees will encounter obstacles, accusations, and persecution. Remember, the race is not given to the swift but to those who endure until the end.

IMPRINT

I teach individuals who have sacrificed their dreams to re-establish their vision and walk in their purpose. As a result, I am looking for individuals who want to empower, encourage, and enlighten others to reach their designed purpose and impactfully touch the world. Whom do you know?

CHAPTER 9

Empowering To Purpose (Inheritance)

Inheritance means conquest, possession, or heritage. It is God's desire that *"A good man leaves an inheritance for his children's children,"* Proverbs 13:22 admonishes, *"It should be everyone's desire to leave an inheritance for the next generation."* Most individuals don't strive to leave an inheritance because it is all about them. It is my desire to leave an inheritance to my children and children's children. I have come to the conclusion that if individuals don't have the mindset to think differently about success, abundance, and prosperity, they will never understand how to leave an inheritance.

I also concluded, that people don't possess the potential in them to accumulate wealth or conquest and how to fulfill purpose to acquire the inheritance to leave. There are seven steps to empowering others to reach their purpose so that they can possess their inheritance:

1. **Assess the individual who you are empowering.**

I find that most people can't handle being empowered because of the authority given. I remember going through this as I worked through the *8-Stages of Spiritual Maturation* with Dr. Trimm.

EMPOWERING TO PURPOSE

She knew that I was not ready to lead the masses as God had promised and she took me step-by-step through the maturation process. She told me that I could be at 100% spiritually, while my finances or relationships could be at 50%. What she meant was that for us to live a life of prosperity or abundance, each area of our lives should be at 100%, or at least close.

It is important to assess the individual before mentoring him or her. Otherwise, the result can frustrate someone who has tremendous experience and is attempting to empower someone who is moving too slowly. Especially, if the mentor does not know why the person is moving slowly.

As one who has experienced the opposite, just after having been ordained by Dr. Trimm's Apostolic Counsel, I thought I was ready to jump right into teaching my online courses and webinars. She told me, "When the student is ready, the teacher will appear." Well, I thought the teacher had already appeared. But what she meant by that is that I was ready in one area of my life. But to be massive or to achieve greatness as God had already promised me, I still had not reached my full potential. As my mentor, she saw that I was not quite ready to be massive.

I had to take one step at a time and not rush God's plan and purpose for my life. Everybody has the potential to succeed, but it is not an overnight event. When empowering others to reach purpose and pull their potential out of their efforts, we must find out what they lack. We must also help develop it and equip them with what they need. Suggested areas include knowledge, skill, and desire.

2. **Empower others with potential by being someone they can imitate.**

As a mentor, the people you are empowering should have someone to look at who has been through the process. Dr. Trimm is my mentor and I have been watching her since 2010. I have been watching her work ethic, her gifts in the ministry to pray with authority and preach and teach with precision, and her ability to allow God to download strategies to create wealth to build His Kingdom. He has also allowed her, in the process, to build and maintain a multi-million-dollar entity.

Another person I have been able to admire, one who has gone from welfare to riches, is Lisa Nichols. She admits to the struggle she and her son encountered by barely making it. However, with her persistence, faith, and desire to live abundantly, she moved past her limitations and pursued abundance in her industry. Lisa was able to build her company, *Motivating the Masses, Inc.*, and become the second African American woman to go public with her company. I can truly say that these two women have empowered me to be successful so that I could empower others as well as leave an inheritance for my children and children's children.

3. **Give those whom you empower permission to succeed.**

No one can make anyone succeed. We all have choices. How badly do you want it? I can remember that I wanted it but didn't know how to succeed. I knew that there was more in me but didn't know how to pull it out of me. I remember telling Dr. Trimm that our spirits were connected and that I had her DNA. I told her that I didn't want anything from her other than for her to pull the potential out of me.

Everyone does not believe he or she can be successful, and it is up to the person empowering to push him or her to success. It is up to the mentor to help those to believe they want to be successful by expecting them to be successful, and verbalizing and reinforcing their success.

I remember after acknowledging to Dr. Trimm my request for her to pull my potential out, she began teaching me her *8 Stages of Spiritual Maturation* process which helped me grow to become successful in all areas of my life. This process allowed me to get clarity of purpose and pursue destiny. When people see that their mentor wants them to succeed, they will begin to believe in themselves and know that they can succeed.

EMPOWERING TO PURPOSE

4. **Transference of authority.**

    As people who empower, mentor, or influence, a sharing or transfer of authority should occur to those we are working to empower. Empowering others is allowing them to develop the ability to work independently under authority.

    I remember Dr. Trimm indicating that she will pray, cover me, and give to me what God has said to her regarding my purpose. She indicated that it was up to me to trust the God in her to receive the instructions. Meeting challenges, solving problems, and becoming strong and effective cannot occur if the opportunity doesn't present itself for the one you are empowering. When you release him or her to act independently, you give him or her the confidence to take authority, accept challenges, and to learn from his or her mistakes.

    "Faith without works is dead." After the knowledge and the strategies are acquired and implanted, there must be action steps. Revelations, dreams, and visions without action steps are simply just dreams, visions, and revelation absorbing your thoughts. To receive knowledge without action is little more than a person walking around with a head full of knowledge. Knowledge is meant to be shared, implemented, or put into action. Purpose is meant to be fulfilled. Destiny is meant to be reached.

5. **Instill confidence in the person you are empowering.**

   Providing the opportunity for public recognition and affirmation lets the student know that you believe in him or her. Such a gesture not only builds confidence in the student, but it also lets others know that you are the one empowering or supporting the him or her. On November 12, 2017, I was grateful because Dr. Trimm and her Apostolic Global Counsel affirmed me by ordaining me. This was a feeling of gratitude, achievement, humbleness, and affirmation. I was earlier ordained in 2006, but this later ordination by my mentor was finally something I could be proud of. My first license and ordination now appeared to me as a mere formality. This ordination by my mentor affirmed that I am who I am; at last I had a leader who believed in me. She believed in the gift in me to reach the world and expand my territory.

   Reflecting over that weekend regarding Dr. Trimm and her Apostolic Global Counsel ordaining me on what God was saying, I saw in my notes that Apostle Les Bowling had said, "Your destiny is linked to a place because God made a place before he made man... As believers, we have authority, but our assignments are territory."

   In Joshua, Chapter 3, God told the Israelites that they had been there three days and that they had to move out of their position and follow the Ark of the Covenant. "Then you will know which way to go."

EMPOWERING TO PURPOSE

I spent three days, November 3-5, 2017, in purpose, and then three more days, November 10-12, 2017, in purpose as well. God is calling some of us to move out of our positions and places of complacency to possess new territory. It is only by His leading that we will get into our assigned territory.

6. **Evaluate the student or mentee.**

   The student or mentee will need to get feedback on his or her mistakes to measure growth. In giving feedback, be positively critical and not judgmental. Give the mentee what he or she needs and not what they want.

   We all have made mistakes and we are all growing and carrying our own measure of faith. I remember back in 2012, I thought Dr. Trimm had become hard in her delivery, so it offended me, and I stopped following her for some years. At the time, I didn't know that all things work out for the good and that maybe if I had stuck it out and received the correction without getting offended, I would be further than where I now am. Thank God that I matured and received her back in my life so that I could continue to grow. I thank God that now my heart is open for correction and rebuke because I know that it was all for my good.

   Nothing remains the same. Even in the complacency of "non-movement," there is change. A plant may stop growing to its potential and eventually, it will wither away. Change is inevitable in the physical body, but internal change depends on our will to change. Jesus grew in wisdom and stature. Growth in God's wisdom will grant us favor with God and with man. We do well when we expand our capacity to be all God wants for us and become open to what He wants to do in us. There are no limits, boundaries, or confinements in the wisdom of God. It is wisdom that attracts reward, brings about promotion, enlargement, esteem, recognition, and concessions. Nothing is impossible with God, but we have to believe to receive the impossible.

7. **Empowering others in their purpose fosters self-reliance.**

This is the step where the mentor releases the student or mentee to make his or her own decisions and to succeed on his or her own. As the mentor or the person empowering, it is our responsibility to release power and ability to the mentee to soar on his or her own. We must to also encourage him or her that we are still available to give assistance if needed. Even while I was writing the last part of this book, Dr. Trimm sent a tweet indicating to me to make sound and solid decisions because one day my future self will thank me.

My goal for 2017 was to empower my grown children to be able to receive the bequest or possession that I will leave them and my grandchildren. I bestowed on my daughter Daria and my son Dave Jr. that they must change their way of thinking to receive the success God wants them to have. The inheritance, in my eyes, is the empowerment to sustain what is left of the person empowering or the mentor.

CONCLUSION

Life will incite us to climb mountains, scale hills, tread over terrains, trample rocky roads, and swim in deep waters. But without life, there will be no journey to reach destiny. So, what is the purpose of life? Jesus said, "In this world will be trouble, but I have overcome." We are overcomers. Life will play us if we let it. Don't let life play you! Transition is changeover, metamorphosis, and progression. There is another side of the mountain, the hill, across the terrain, and out of the deep into the shallow. Learn to embrace the ride of life. Enjoy the sailing of purpose and take the limitations off succeeding in life. Nothing is impossible with God. I decree increase and faith. I decree expansion of the mind.

DECLARATION AND AFFIRMATIONS!

- I am who God says I am. I am the salt of the earth and a light that illuminates the world.
- I am fearfully and wonderfully made. (Psalm 139:14)
- I am made in the image of God; therefore, I have dominion and power.
- I am healed.
- I am delivered.
- I am wealthy.
- I am prosperous.
- I am successful.
- I choose to live holy.
- I choose to live righteous.
- I choose to walk in dominion.
- I choose life.
- I choose to bless others with my wealth.
- I choose to take authority over the enemy coming against me to try to steal my purpose.
- I choose long life.
- I choose to think in the positive.
- I choose Godly decisions for my life.
- I choose abundance in every area of my life.
- I choose the unfamiliar to expand my territory.

- I choose a greater capacity to reach my destiny. I choose to walk in purpose.
- I choose long life for my children and children's children.

Choose you this day whom you will serve.

Remember that knowing thy own self will refute negative belief systems which can grab your destiny, but the truth of who you were really created to be will catapult you into your designed purpose and destiny.

NOTES

1. APS. (2013). *Diagnostic and Statistical Manual of Mental Disorders.* American Psychiatric Publishing 5th Ed. 1000 Wilson Boulevard, Suite 1825, Arlington, VA., 22209-3901.
2. Goodreads. *Popular Quotes.* htttps://www.goodreads.com/quotes
3. Maxwell, John. (1997). *Becoming a Person of Influence.* Maxwell Motivation, Inc. Thomas Nelson, Inc. Publishers. Nashville, Tennessee.
4. Nichols, Lisa. (2016). *Abundance Now.* HarperCollins Publishers, 195 Broadway, New York, NY. 10007.
5. NIV. (1984). *The Holy Bible, New International Version.* Zondervan, International Bible Society.

ABOUT THE AUTHOR

I am Tanja P. Hightower, the CEO of Tanja P. Hightower International, 3 Es, reaching purpose and touching the world where we empower, encourage, and enlighten individuals through inspirational/transformational speaking, mentoring, blogging, and transformational workshops and courses.

As a result of what I do, people will be introduced to the person they were created to be and find purpose. They will reach their full potential and expand their capacity to become successful while fulfilling purpose. We are all on a journey. We all have a purpose, we all have a journey that is a part of purpose. I am here to help you grab hold of your destiny and jump-start the journey. I'm looking for individuals who are open-minded to creative thinking and ready to grab hold of their desired purpose, destiny and dream. Are you ready for greatness? Will you grab your destiny to reach the abundant life that has been destined for you?

As the CEO of Tanja P. Hightower International, I am a speaker, mentor, teacher, preacher, author, and life transformer. I have two master's degrees, one in Clinical Mental Health Counseling and the other in Divinity. I also have a Doctor of Divinity degree. I was a Health Inspector, Parole Officer, and Adult Protective Services Specialist. I am a licensed ordained minister who has served in ministry for 20 years. I was an Associate Basketball Coach and a Mentor in the Katy School District. I was also a member of the American Counseling Association.

Among all the accomplishments and achievements that I have obtained, none of them means anything if I don't know who I am and why I was put on this earth. It means nothing if I don't know my purpose and do not allow my life to grab its destiny. My purpose is to do what I am doing now and what I love to do.

I empower, encourage, and enlighten others to be who they were created to be, to know their identity, why they were put on this earth, and how to fulfill their purpose whether through personal development or business acumen. I am charged to reach beyond the mundane of the church, making disciples and empowering the world to fulfill purpose and to grab hold of their destiny.

We will embark on this journey together because I am still grabbing my destiny. Destiny is a journey, and there are pit stops, detours, fast lanes, slow lanes in which all play a part in reaching or grabbing destiny, but we are not alone.

Hold onto your seat, buckle up, and let's take this journey together.

Connect with Dr. Tanja Hightower

If we were created with purpose and created in the Divine's image, then the only One that can give us our identity is the One who created us. Moreover, the only One who knows our destiny is the Creator. If we want to know our purpose and destiny, then we must be connected to the source of creation, the One that can give us direction, instructions, and revelation of our destiny. John Ruskin stated, "Every person confronts three great questions. Where am I from? Whether am I going? And what must I do on the way?"

Available at amazon.com BARNES&NOBLE www.bn.com

Follow Me @tphightowerint f 🐦

For more products and services, visit www.tphightowerint.com

www.ingramcontent.com/pod-product-compliance
Lightning Source LLC
Chambersburg PA
CBHW052200110526
44591CB00012B/2023